THE LOVE ISSUE

What is LOVE?

In this issue, we spotlight friendships, families, hobbies, fan clubs, and best-loved books. Famous duos of kidlit reveal love in action, a poet ponders where love resides, and artists discuss the bittersweet joys of collaboration. Learn to say "love" in another language, send anonymous valentines, and make fairy bread for your bestie.

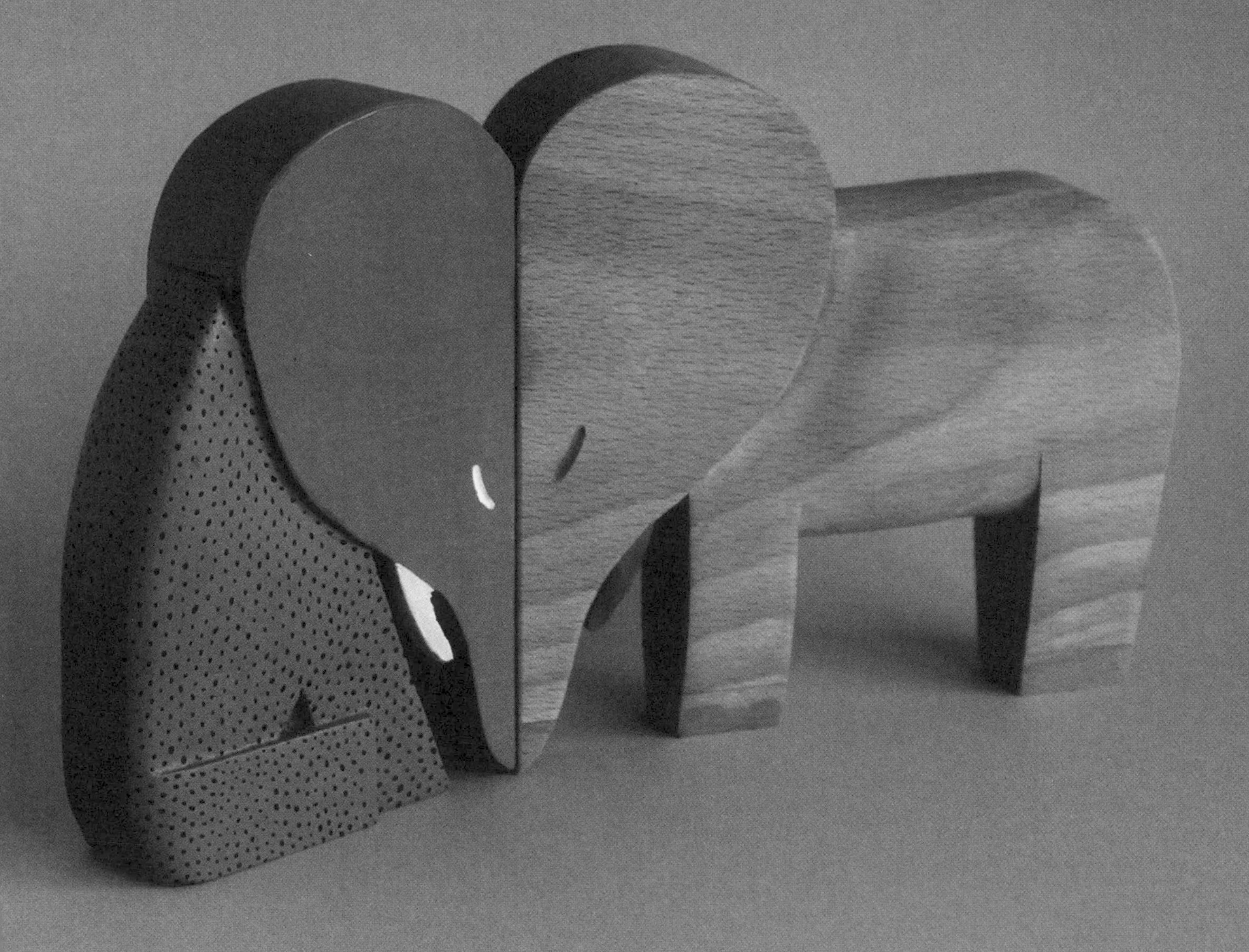

FROM US TO YOU...

IN EVERY ISSUE WE ASK OUR CONTRIBUTORS A QUESTION.
FOR THE LOVE ISSUE, WE WONDERED:
If you could be president of a fan club for something you love, what would it be?

edible things

SANDWICH FAN CLUB
Italian chapter = Panino Club
(Elenia)

MAYONNAISE FAN CLUB
(Jillian)

"Tagliatelle della Nonna" FAN CLUB
(Italian for "Grandma's Noodles")
(Valerio)

MUSHROOM FAN CLUB
(Tom)

PICKLE CLUB
(Amy)

cute things

STUFFED ANIMAL FAN CLUB
(Golden Cosmos)

CHUBBY CATERPILLAR APPRECIATION CLUB
(Pix)

THE COLOMBIAN FLOWERS FAN CLUB
(Alejandra)

contributors:

JESSIXA & AARON BAGLEY, ALEX ALDRICH BARRETT, KATIE BENN, ELENIA BERETTA, TOM BINGHAM, CHIAOZZA, GOLDEN COSMOS, KELLETTE ELLIOT, YUK FUN, ANIS MOJGANI, ALEJANDRA OVIEDO, WENG PIXIN, EMILY RASMUSSEN, AMY SUMERTON, JILLIAN TAMAKI, ELEVATOR TEETH, VALERIO VIDALI, & LARRY PEACE-LOVE YES

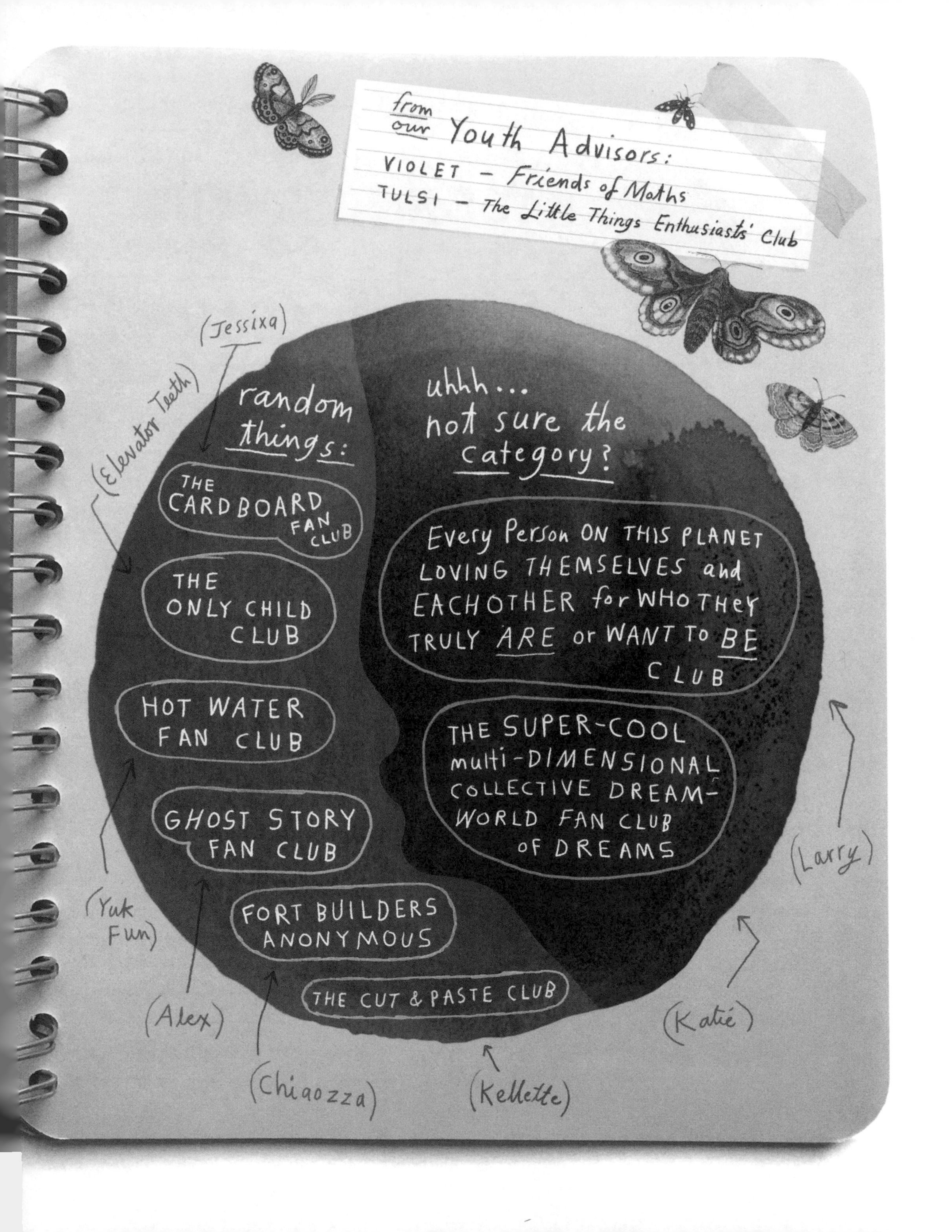
from our Youth Advisors:
VIOLET – Friends of Moths
TULSI – The Little Things Enthusiasts' Club
random things:
uhhh... not sure the category?
THE CARDBOARD FAN CLUB
THE ONLY CHILD CLUB
HOT WATER FAN CLUB
GHOST STORY FAN CLUB
FORT BUILDERS ANONYMOUS
THE CUT & PASTE CLUB
Every Person ON THIS PLANET LOVING THEMSELVES and EACHOTHER for WHO THEY TRULY ARE or WANT TO BE CLUB
THE SUPER-COOL multi-DIMENSIONAL COLLECTIVE DREAM-WORLD FAN CLUB OF DREAMS
(Jessixa)
(Elevator Teeth)
(Yuk Fun)
(Alex)
(Chiaozza)
(Kellette)
(Katie)
(Larry)

MEET SPECIAL GUESTS

cover artist
VALERIO VIDALI

guest writers
JESSIXA AND AARON BAGLEY

guest poet
ANIS MOJGANI

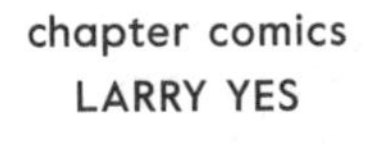

chapter comics
LARRY YES

typographic artist
ELEVATOR TEETH

CHAPTER 1

LAUGH AND PLAY

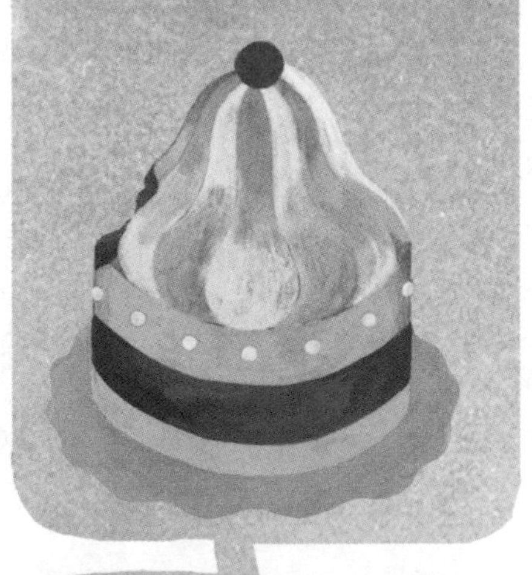

GRAB A FRIEND AND TRY THESE!

CHAPTER 2

READ AND LEARN

CHAPTER 3

DRAW, WRITE, MAKE

CHAPTER 4

LOOK AND LISTEN

EXTRAS

DEEPER DIVE

THE LOVE ISSUE

ILLUSTORIA IS THE OFFICIAL PUBLICATION OF THE INTERNATIONAL ALLIANCE OF YOUTH WRITING CENTERS

LOVE
YOUR
SELF

LAUGH & PLAY

OUR CHAPTER PAGES FEATURE ART BY LARRY YES (LEFT) AND ELEVATOR TEETH (RIGHT).

WORD SLEUTH

TYPOGRAPHIC ART BY EMILY RASMUSSEN

SEARCH FOR LOVE AND ALL OF ITS MANY FORMS

FIND

- EMPATHY
- RESPECT
- CARING
- FRIENDSHIP
- LOVE
- VIBES

```
            P G S E R
        C X S D E M M Z U
      B E S S H E Z V P Y Y
    R U N C A R I N G T A T X
    D K D U T Y F R L C S T I
  F F E X T Z E X E M D V I H R
  U R U G L D G Q S L Q I F Q Y
  K S I A X W A E P O R B B V N
  P P O E W V K V E V H E K F I
  E Q W Y N H G F C E W S G Y T
    M G U L D D X T X L R M W
    X Y K T Q S B G W P Z Q F
      K L O G P H H Z A J S
        F I S O Y I T N J
            C J J W P
```

FRENCH
Amour

SOYAYYA
Hausa

AMAR
Spanish

munay
QUECHUA

amor
Portuguese

MUNAÑA
Aymara

mborayhu
GUARANI

Icelandic
ELSKA
GERMAN
Liebe
Любовь
(RUSSIAN)
Bengali
ভালবাসা
хайр
mongolian
RAKKAUS
FINNISH
miłość
Polish
LJUBAV
(BOSNIAN)
사랑
KOREAN
ELSKER
danish
ROMANIAN
махаббат
kazakh
爱
CHINESE
DRAGOSTE
arabic
حب
प्रेम
nepali
รัก
Thai
AŞK
Turkish
ayl
SomALI
UPENDO
SWAHILI
gbo
thando
xhosa
CINTA
Indonesian
Here's how the rest of the world says "LOVE"

Story Starters

by Amy Sumerton

WHAT I/YOU/SHE/HE/THEY LOVE(S)

SOMETHING WRITERS DO

Sometimes writers write from the point of view of characters, and sometimes these characters are very different from the writers themselves. Part of what makes writing such a fun game is imagining how other people think and feel... and what they LOVE! For this writing game, we've gathered some images related to highly-specific interests and professions. What point of view will you use?

FOLLOW THESE STEPS

When we say "write" we mean that word b r o a d l y! Writing includes telling the story aloud, through drawings, by collaborating with others, and by actually putting words on paper with a pencil. How will YOU tell this story?

- Cut out the cards on the opposite page, turn them over, and shuffle.

- Pull one card. Write a paragraph or two from a character who LOVES doing this. Explain why they love it and what they love about it.

- Pull another card. Now, add a couple of paragraphs from the character from your first paragraph when they discover this new interest (which, it turns out, they ALSO LOVE).

- Pull another card. Write a few more paragraphs about what happens when they combine these interests.

POINT OF VIEW

First person: stories that use the pronoun I or WE
example: "I loved building bridges..."

Second person: stories that use the pronoun YOU
example: "You loved designing anti-gravity shoes..."

Third person: stories that use the pronouns SHE, HE, THEY
example: "She loved building bridges to planets with intense gravitational fields, where her futuristic hover-heel shoes could be put to use..."

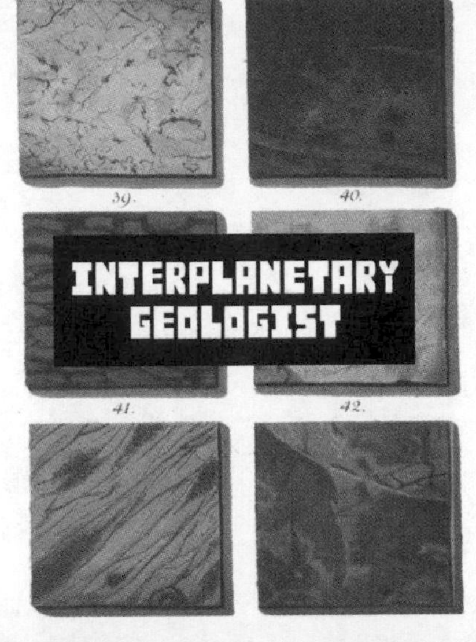

TIRE-SWING ENGINEER

ANTI-GRAVITY SHOE DESIGNER

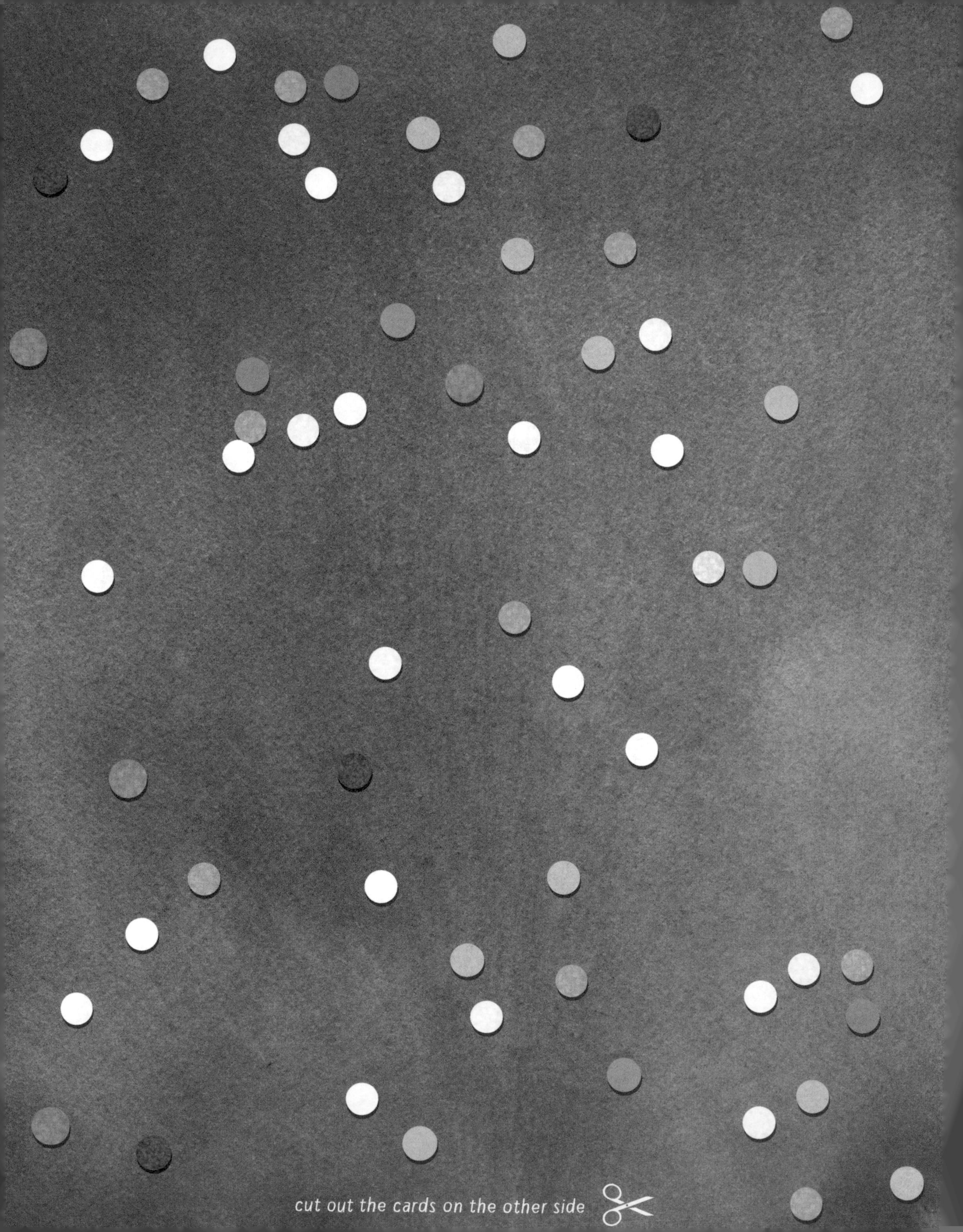
cut out the cards on the other side

KIDS LOVE SWEET THINGS!

One study showed that adults tend to max out their sugar tolerance at about the level of sugar in a can of soda, but older children still liked drinks that were twice as sweet. What about younger children? The scientists couldn't find a limit to the concentration of sugar they preferred. Newborns were found to have a higher concentration of taste buds that are receptive to sweet tastes, making them more receptive to their mothers' milk. This is something shared by children globally, across cultures and climates. Having a sweet tooth is truly a universal thing!

DODGE THE SWEET FLAVORS

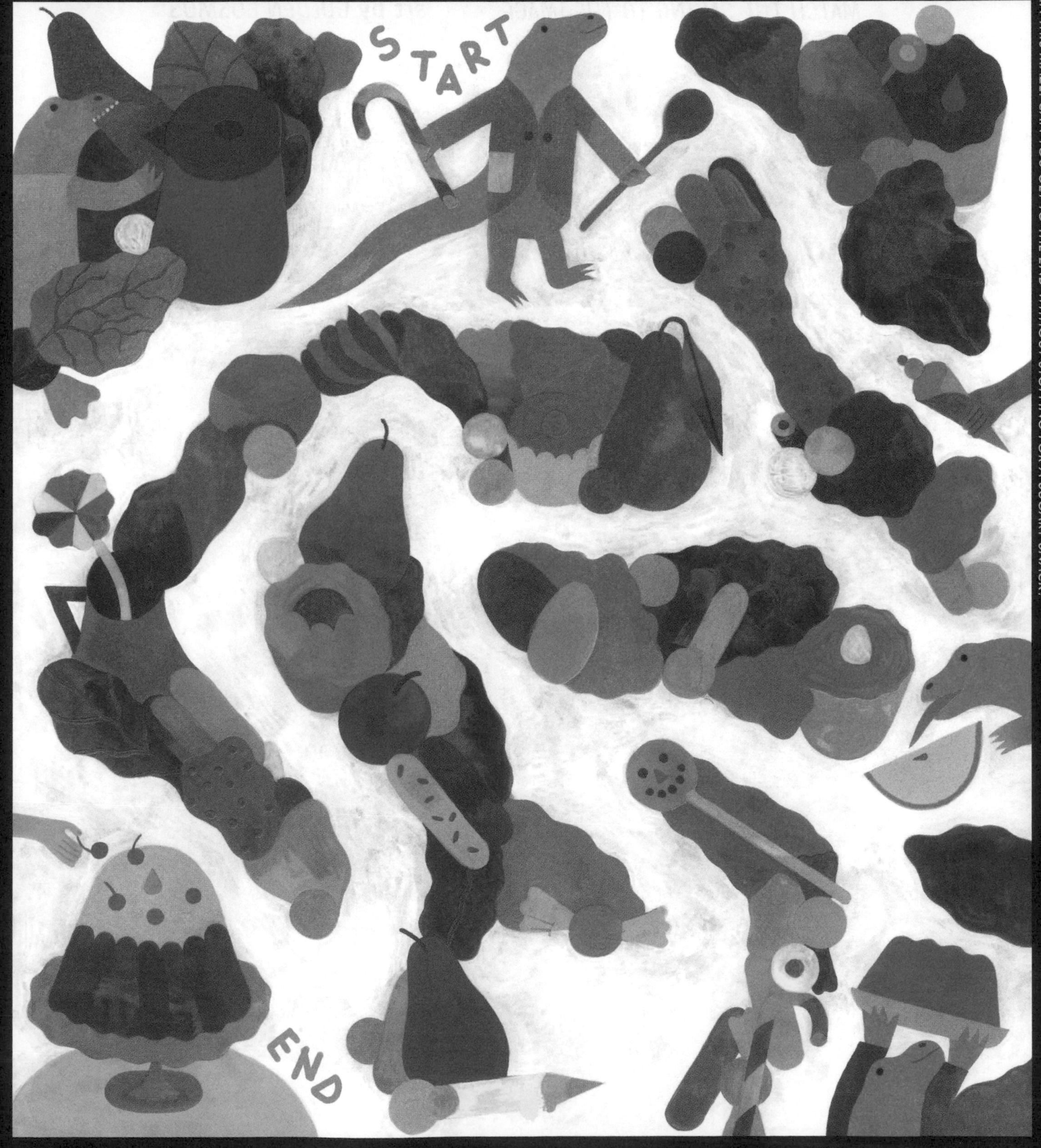

art by ELENIA BERETTA

MATCH THE SAYING TO THE IMAGE

art by GOLDEN COSMOS

For some reason, I find you so appealing.

We've gone round and round about it... We can't put our finger on it, but we just DIG each other...

Doggone it, you're the only one I can say anything to.

Gotta brush up on my manners when I hear that you're coming over for dinner.

Time spent with you is... how shall I say... uplifting?

Shid I eveh shay I blub you...?

UNLIKELY ANIMAL FRIENDSHIPS

SOMETIMES LOVE IS UNPREDICTABLE. YOU NEVER KNOW WHEN A BOND MIGHT FORM, EVEN AMONG OPPOSITES. SOME ANIMAL PAIRS ARE SURPRISING... ESPECIALLY WHEN PREDATORS COZY UP TO THEIR PREY!

WHATEVER THE REASON, THESE UNEXPECTED FRIENDSHIPS PULL AT OUR HEARTSTRINGS. IF A CHEETAH AND A PUPPY CAN BECOME BUDS, PERHAPS WORLD PEACE IS WITHIN REACH?

GLADYS CHICKEN AND SNOWY THE CAT

Gladys, a rescued chicken in Suffolk, England, found an unlikely ally in Snowy the cat. Snowy often grooms Gladys, and the pair refuse to go outside without each other.

THEMBA THE ELEPHANT AND ALBERT THE SHEEP

In a South African wildlife reserve, an orphaned elephant named Themba became besties with Albert the sheep. They are now inseparable and even eat the same food!

MZEE THE TORTOISE AND OWEN THE HIPPOPOTAMUS

Mzee the tortoise is 130 years older than Owen, a baby hippopotamus. Owen was rescued from a tsunami in 2004 and brought to an animal sanctuary in Kenya. As soon as he arrived, the baby hippo ran and hid behind the giant tortoise, and the two have been inseparable ever since.

MADE WITH LOVE

WRITERS AND ARTISTS INSPIRED BY LOVE

ELEANOR ROOSEVELT

Activist and former first lady of the United States Eleanor Roosevelt was orphaned at age 8 and found a mentor in Marie Souvestre, the headmistress at her boarding school. Souvestre inspired Roosevelt to think independently and have confidence in herself. Roosevelt, famous for her letters, wrote to her mentor until the day she died.

FRIDA KAHLO

Mexican painter Frida Kahlo was incredibly close with her father. Guillermo Kahlo was a photographer and encouraged Frida to pursue a career as an artist. She painted a portrait called *Portrait of My Father* and signed it, "...with adoration, his daughter Frida Kahlo."

UTAGAWA KUNIYOSHI

Japanese engraver Utagawa Kuniyoshi was influenced by his love of cats! He would often work with a kitten snuggled up in his kimono. The woodblock print *Cats Suggested as the Fifty-Three Stations of the Tōkaidō* has fifty-five cats and dozens of cat puns in it.

BELL HOOKS

American author bell hooks was deeply inspired by her maternal great-grandmother and adopted her pen name (in lowercase) as an homage to her great-grandmother's "snappy and bold tongue." She taught bell that sisterhood empowers women by respecting, protecting, encouraging, and loving them—a belief system that she instilled into her writing.

ANDY WARHOL

American pop artist Andy Warhol greatly loved and admired his mother, Julia Warhola. Julia was also an artist and hand-lettered many of Andy's illustrated books.

In 1960 they created a book together featuring Julia's calligraphy alongside her cat and angel drawings.

Andy made a portrait series called *Julia Warhola* and a movie called *Mrs. Warhol*, immortalizing her forever.

LOVE
EACH
OTHER

READ & LEARN

OUR CHAPTER PAGES FEATURE ART BY **LARRY YES** (LEFT) AND **ELEVATOR TEETH** (RIGHT)

FAMOUS DUOS
OF CHILDREN'S LITERATURE

by guest writers: *Jessixa and Aaron Bagley*

So there are two mice, Hunca Munca and Tom Thumb. One day they sneak into a dollhouse and find a bunch of delicious-looking food. A beautiful shiny ham, a lovely piece of fish, lobster, oranges... But, when they try to eat it, they realize it's all fake! WHAT?!

They try with all their might to figure out what's up with the food, but in the process absolutely DESTROY everything in the dollhouse.

OF COURSE they shouldn't have done that, but what is really great is how they are both there for each other no matter what. In adventure, in distress, in unplanned destruction, and ultimately in repairing the damage they've caused! They truly have each other's back through thick and thin.

I mean, that's real love right?

Chirri and Chirra are two sisters who happen to get along with each other. While riding bicycles, they find themselves suddenly miniaturized and exploring impossible places underground—deep in the sea, in the dark of night.

Chirri and Chirra remind us that fantasy worlds are even more astounding with a companion, because when it's over, you shared it with your bestie and that fact makes it real.

Never has emotion been personified better than in Tinker Bell, especially where companionship is concerned. As a fairy, Tinker Bell is limited to one emotion at a time. But whether she is angry, curious, or joyful... she's 100% loyal, even risking her life to save Peter.

Friends don't wait until they are in the 'mood' to be there for you. TRUE friendship is steadfast, no matter the complicated emotions at hand.

the creators of this BOOK about the ups and downs of sibling rivalry and friendship, talk about THEIR FAVORITE duos in beloved picture books.

DUEL
"I love this book. . . . En garde!" —Victoria Jamieson, New York Times bestselling author of Roller Girl
WRITTEN BY JESSIXA BAGLEY
ILLUSTRATED BY AARON BAGLEY

Two seemingly similar creatures who couldn't be more DIFFERENT: a frog and a toad. Okay, technically those are VERY similar. But in this case, one is joyful, optimistic, and grateful. The other is self-conscious, worrisome... stressed out. Opposites can make the best of friends when they appreciate your differences. That's the beauty of Frog and Toad—all love and no judgment!

Their unwavering friendship got them through lost buttons, bad dreams, and some... ahem... questionable swimsuit decisions. If there are two characters who inspired the phrase "BFF," they are definitely Frog and Toad.

FOREWORD BY
JULIA DONALDSON

Frog and Toad

ARNOLD LOBEL

THE COMPLETE COLLECTION

DORA FOLLOWS HER PASSION
BY YUK FUN
I'VE LOVED POTTERY EVER SINCE I WAS SMALL
GRANDPA USED TO MAKE LOVELY VASES IN HIS SHED...
GRANDPA
YOUNG DORA
SO A FEW MONTHS AGO I DID A CERAMICS COURSE
AND NOW I MAKE FUN TEAPOTS LIKE THIS
THERE ARE SO MANY THINGS I LOVE ABOUT MAKING TEAPOTS! DRAWING MY IDEAS...
THROWING ON THE WHEEL...
PAINTING THE GLAZE...
AND FIRING IN THE KILN
AH... SO WARM
MY HORSE FRIEND SAID I SHOULD SELL THEM
YOU'D MAKE A TON OF MONEY!
AND I'D BE DOING SOMETHING I LOVE!
SO I SPENT MY SAVINGS ON MATERIALS AND EQUIPMENT...
£300
Clay Town
SET UP A WEBSITE...
DORA'S DREAMPOTS
AND NOW I SELL MY POTS ONLINE AND AT FAIRS!
WWW.DREAM
DORA'S

TODAY I'M DOING A MARKET!
CERAMAGIC
T-POTS
SO KIND!
THESE TEAPOTS BRING ME SUCH JOY! I'LL BUY THREE
THIS IS WEIRD AND EXPENSIVE
OH
LATER
SO TIRED
EVEN LATER
JUST GOT ONE MORE ORDER TO PACK...
LATER STILL
I WAS GOING TO TAKE TOMORROW OFF
PING
EMAIL FROM: THE MAYOR
I'VE BEEN ASKED TO MAKE A FOUNTAIN FOR THE TOWN SQUARE!
POW
SPLAT
CRACK
OOPS!
WIPE
DORA, YOU DID A GREAT JOB!
DORA?
MAYOR
DORA?
THE END

WE ASKED A POET

ANIS MOJGANI IS THE POET LAUREATE OF OREGON. WE ASKED HIM TO TELL US ABOUT LOVE. HERE ARE HIS THOUGHTS.

art by ALEJANDRA OVIEDO

All my heart
does is love.
It'll love anything.
It loves everything.

It's my brain and my body that sometimes leads it elsewhere.

It's the three of them–Heart, Brain, Body– carrying me through this rough and tumble glorious hard and beautiful world.

And I don't know why this is.

I know about my brain and my body, but my heart, I keep trying to figure out.

Or at least my brain keeps trying to figure my heart out.

Heart is happy being Heart.

Brain often is talking so loudly to Heart–

"HEART I LOVE YOU AND I DON'T WANT ANYTHING TO HAPPEN TO YOU"

While Heart says nothing, just smiles and keeps pulling Body towards a sunset to share with Brain

the colors the sun spills across a sky...

Not really concerned with how close to the edge of the Earth it might be pulling us–

Heart only wants to marvel and share the marvelous things the world loves all of us with.

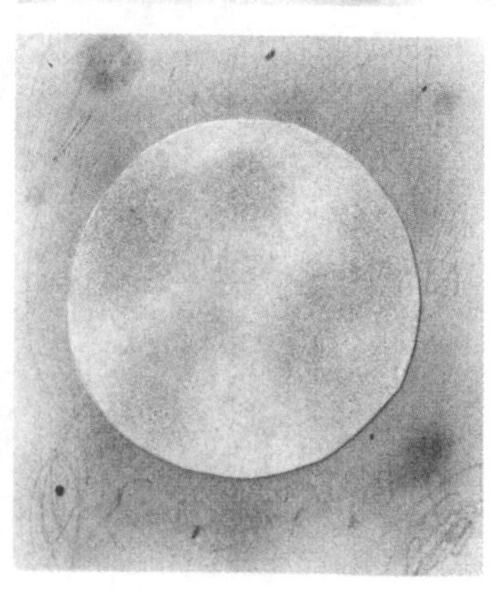

Brain yells
"HEART DO YOU NOT SEE HOW CLOSE TO THE EDGE OF THIS CLIFF YOU ARE BRINGING US JUST TO SHARE A SUNSET?"
Body says nothing too, smiles, tries to gentle Brain, letting Brain know that Body won't let us fall over
...helps Heart to bring Brain closer to what is beautiful, closer to what Heart loves, closer to what Heart knows Brain and Body will love too.
And Brain, as loud and worried as Brain sometimes is, loves Heart.
And so sometimes, Brain quiets enough to do this–to let Heart lead the others to what is loved, and to sit with Heart and Body,
and love alongside them too.

SYNANTHROPE: ONE-SIDED LOVE?

words by Amy Sumerton art by Julie Benbassat

How about one-sided love, when feelings of admiration are not returned? Take synanthropes—organisms that have chosen to live closely with humans to benefit from them. Many might assume that synanthropes are just thinking of themselves and their own needs, yet these creatures live closely with humans because it increases their chances of survival. We don't need them, but they have become dependent on us. A raccoon, for example, looks through our garbage for food... but what if that raccoon actually felt love for the humans whose leftovers it ate? We imagined some odes that our favorite urban creature companions might write to their favorite humans.

Oh humans, how I adore you! Always with the most beautiful bobbles and always tossing them about! Loves, don't ever change! My heart! Is that a dime?

CROW

- *Extremely intelligent*
- *Mate for life*
- *Very social, family-oriented birds*
- *Can remember human faces (and will bring gifts to people they like or hold a grudge)*

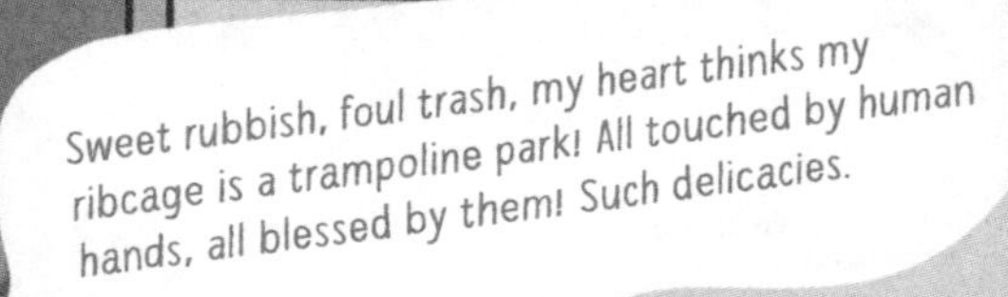

Sweet rubbish, foul trash, my heart thinks my ribcage is a trampoline park! All touched by human hands, all blessed by them! Such delicacies.

RACCOON

- *Opportunistic eaters, which means they feed on whatever is most convenient*
- *Highly adaptable*
- *Front and hind paws have five digits*
- *Primarily crepuscular (active at dawn and dusk) and nocturnal (active at night)*

Don't just take from love–one must make deposits too! I tend the plants as I tend the garden of my love for you, dear humans. My species has loved you across many eons.

COCKROACH

- Can live without a head for up to a week
- Originated more than 280 million years ago
- Over 4,000 species worldwide
- Can run up to three miles an hour (that's fast for such short legs!)

We've loved you such a long time, oh humans! We watched you evolve, and loved you before time had even been invented. We will patiently love alongside you for as long as you exist.

GINKGO TREE

- Its leaves famously turn golden all at once, producing a "leaf dump" on a single day in October
- No known relatives, making them living fossils that have been essentially unchanged for more than 200 million years
- Their iconic fan-shaped leaves have been identified in fossils on every continent

PROCESS *interview*

COLLABORATIVE DUOS:

how do you COMBINE artistic forces?

PHOTO CREDITS, FROM TOP: NIKITA TERYOSHIN, MIKE VORRASI, @ITSNOTANOTHERSHOT, LEE DILLON*
*COURTESY OF R. MICHELSON GALLERIES, REPRESENTING THE DILLON'S ARTWORK

ABOVE: *LUMPY NOTES* - INSTALLED AT NORTHEASTERN UNIVERSITY IN BOSTON

CHIAOZZA IS THE COMBINED NAME OF TERRI CHIAO AND ADAM FREZZA, AN AMERICAN ARTIST DUO BASED IN NYC. TOGETHER THEY EXPLORE PLAY AND CRAFT ACROSS A RANGE OF MEDIA, SUCH AS PAINTINGS, SCULPTURE, INSTALLATION, COLLAGE, AND PHOTOGRAPHY.

What's the meaning behind your name, as an artistic duo?

CHIAOZZA (pronounced "CHOW-zah," rhymes with "wowza") is a combination of our last names, CHIAO and FREZZA. We like that it's fun to say, and also that it's direct and it's who we are.

If there's conflict while working, what helps you find harmony again?

When we have disagreements, we try to remember that what we've created together is unique. We value each other's ideas, especially when they are different.

What's an upside and a downside to the experience of working together?

An upside to working together is that we get to hang out all the time making fun projects, which we enjoy. Growing our ideas together also helps take them to places we might not arrive to on our own.

A downside is that it can be hard to piece together a living as artists–it's a sport to balance creative output with the business side of things, not to mention the addition of parenting!

Any advice for others who wish to try a collaboration?

For any collaboration to be successful, there must be a foundation of mutual respect and trust, and a willingness to listen and try new things.

DORIS FREIGOFAS AND DANIEL DOLZ LIVE IN BERLIN AND CREATE UNDER THE NAME GOLDEN COSMOS. THEIR ART WALKS THE LINE BETWEEN A DAYDREAM AND THE EVERYDAY. THEY MANAGE TO WORK WHILE THEIR TWO YOUNG SONS RUN AROUND.

How did you come up with your name, as an artistic duo?

The name Golden Cosmos was inspired by a title of a book: an animal and plant encyclopedia from the 90s. A book about diversity and about the richness and creativity of nature.

Since we're two individuals with distinct styles and a wide range of interests... we thought our name would need to imply all that.

There's no limit in cosmos and creativity is unlimited in Golden Cosmos. And of course our name needed to sound cool :-)

If there's conflict, what helps to 'clear the air' and get back to a harmonious working vibe?

What helped us to avoid conflicts in the first place is not being at the same place 24/7. We work from different places most of the time, one from home and one from the studio. We share desks but take turns... taking a few hours to ourselves is not a bad idea, and helps the working relationship!

Tell us about an upside and a downside to your process.

After working together for almost 15 years we think the upsides clearly outweigh the downsides. It's great to have someone to show your work to and get feedback from. With time, we have found a respectful way of offering criticism when listening to each other. This is also a downside: it's hard to accept criticism!

Any advice for artists who wish to try collaborating?

Do it! It doesn't have to be forever. It can be for a project or just for fun. Found collectives! We all have the same struggles and the same questions; when we unite we are stronger!

Our best advice is to not take yourself too seriously and learn how to listen to others' ideas.

PHOTO CREDIT: KALEIDO SHOOTS

LUCY CHEUNG AND PATRICK GILDERSLEEVES MAKE UP THE DUO KNOWN AS YUK FUN. THEY SPECIALIZE IN SCREEN PRINTING, MASK-MAKING, AND UNBELIEVABLY FUN SWEATSUITS. THEY ARE FREQUENT SPEAKERS AT CONFERENCES, TALKING ABOUT PROCESS AND CRAFT.

How did you come up with your name, as an artistic duo?

Lucy's Chinese middle name is Yuk-Foung, so we took the first bit and changed the second part to "FUN" because we thought it sounded good. "Yuk" means "to bring" so we are bringing the fun!

What's a favorite project of yours?

Our favorite would be the Lunar New Year cards that we make every year. We've been making them since 2018, so we've done the years of the dog, pig, rat, ox, tiger and dragon. They are really fun to design and we donate a portion of the proceeds to charity.

Tell us about some of the ups and downs of the collaboration process.

Upside: two heads are better than one! We bounce ideas off each other and come up with solutions to tricky problems. It's good to be able to discuss the big decisions with someone else.

Downside: driving each other up the wall sometimes! We live and work together and in busy periods we're working evenings and weekends. We get on incredibly well, which is lucky, but we do have to know when to give each other space.

Any advice for artists who wish to try collaborating?

Be prepared to adapt and change to work harmoniously with the other artist. Don't be afraid to give and accept constructive criticism. Otherwise, it probably won't work!

If there's conflict while working together, what helps to "clear the air"?

Long and painful hours of silence.

Just joking! We talk things over, it always helps. And a big hug!

ART FROM THE COVER OF
TO EVERYTHING A SEASON

LEO AND DIANE DILLON ARE AMONG THE MOST TALENTED AND VERSATILE ILLUSTRATORS IN THE UNITED STATES. THEIR WORK HAS BEEN AN OUTSTANDING CONTRIBUTION TO CHILDREN OF ALL RACES AND CULTURES. THEY WERE THE FIRST ARTISTS TO BE AWARDED TWO CALDECOTT MEDALS IN ROW.

*Q: The two of you collaborate on each illustration, creating what you call a "third artist." Please explain how this works...?**

DIANE: The third artist is the combination of Leo and me together. It's a combination of the two of us who does something that neither one of us could do separately.

The third artist concept took a big load off of our shoulders, because we then realized we should leave that third artist to do what it does, and not interfere or try to pull it back to what our separate visions are. Our collaboration is worth all of the trouble it caused in working it out.

We had a hard time at first. Like with anything good, there are rocky times. We had our arguments over how we saw a piece being done.

But we learned over the years that there's more than one way to do something. It took years to learn how to do that. It didn't just happen. We learned by trial and error. We found we would sit at the table talking about a manuscript and both agreeing with each other, but when one of us started it, it wasn't at all what the other one was thinking.

So a lot of the initial way we were working was trying to pull the images back to our own concept, and there was always this pulling. It's great having someone who can come over and say, "That's beautiful, but that finger is too long." And now the hairs on the back of our neck might bristle, but it's comforting to know that there's another pair of eyes that can see something, not let it go by, and make it come to life. After almost 50 years, we still have a lot to say to each other.

LEO: We gave away our separate styles with "the Third Artist," and in doing so realized that we opened ourselves to every style that ever existed on the face of the earth. We try to fit our style to the story that goes with it.

When we decided to get married, we realized that we wouldn't last a week if we didn't collaborate because we knew what competitive natures we had after our years together at art school.

So we began to embark on a specific program to discover how two people can work together. We always believed that life is a technique; this was simply another technique to learn. After working together almost 50 years, collaborating is easier than working by ourselves. We always have a friend to lean on, so we can embark on anything.

EARTH MOTHER
Ellen Jackson
Leo & Diane Dillon
Nancy White Carlstrom
NORTHERN LULLABY
Illustrated by Leo and Diane Dillon
HONEY, I LOVE
and other love poems
by Eloise Greenfield
pictures by Diane and Leo Dillon
THE PEOPLE COULD FLY
American Black Folktales
told by VIRGINIA HAMILTON
Illustrated by LEO and DIANE DILLON
Why Mosquitoes Buzz in People's Ears
Verna Aardema
pictures by Leo and Diane Dillon
HER STORIES
African American Folktales, Fairy Tales, and True Tales
told by VIRGINIA HAMILTON
illustrated by LEO & DIANE DILLON
If Kids Ran the World
by LEO & DIANE DILLON
The
SECRET RIVER
MARJORIE KINNAN RAWLINGS
LEO & DIANE DILLON
MAMA SAYS
A Book of Love for Mothers and Sons
ROB D. WALKER • LEO & DIANE DILLON
PARENTS' CHOICE
HONORS
pish, posh,
said
Hieronymus Bosch
BY NANCY WILLARD

ILLUSTRATIONS BY THE DILLONS

YOUTH VOICES
"Collaboration is at the heart of everything I do."

ASHTON MOTA (HE/HIM/ÉL) IS AN AFRO-LATINO YOUTH ACTIVIST, AUTHOR, AND STUDENT AT YALE UNIVERSITY. HE RECENTLY CO-AUTHORED *A KIDS BOOK ABOUT BEING INCLUSIVE*, ALONGSIDE REBEKAH BRUESEHOFF, PUBLISHED BY THE GENDERCOOL PROJECT. ASHTON AIMS TO FOSTER STRONG CONNECTIONS BETWEEN DIVERSE COMMUNITIES THROUGH THE POWER OF STORYTELLING.

WHAT WAS REWARDING AND CHALLENGING ABOUT WRITING *A KIDS BOOK ABOUT BEING INCLUSIVE*?

I love this question! Writing was incredibly rewarding, as it allowed me to create a resource that celebrates and fosters understanding in young readers. I wish I had this as a kid, but I am grateful to be able to share it with others now. However, the process challenged me to further my own self-reflection, confronting areas where I could increase my sense of inclusivity.

WHAT WAS THE PROCESS LIKE?

Writing this book was an enriching experience because of the many meaningful conversations with my co-author, Rebekah, folks from the *A Kids Book About Being Inclusive* and GenderCool team, and discussions and reflections on the experiences our intersectional communities often share.

With conversation at the forefront of our process, we explored the depths of inclusivity by sharing personal stories to broaden our collective understanding. Inclusivity comes down to just that: choosing to try to understand. Through storytelling, we aimed to foster empathy and acceptance in young readers.

WHY IS COLLABORATION IMPORTANT TO YOU?

Collaboration is at the heart of everything I do because it adds meaning to my progress. Throughout my journey as an activist, I've found that nothing could have been achieved without the love, support, and collaboration of my extended family and fellow community leaders. It reminds us that we can't do everything alone and that we are stronger and capable of achieving great things together.

TELL US ABOUT A MENTOR INFLUENCE.

My chosen family; that is to say, my friends, family, and people who I've met along my journey, have had a tremendous influence on my path. Without them, I wouldn't be who I am or advocate the way I do today. One person whom I've consistently considered a distant mentor and representation of the type of person I want to be is Trevor Noah. At first I was drawn to his witty remarks and presence as a Black man in the media, but over time I've grown to admire much more than that.

In his book *Born a Crime*, Trevor writes, "True strength comes from having the courage to be vulnerable and authentic," which I use as a guide and reminder that the depth of my understanding of the world is only as profound as my understanding of myself. This perspective has maximized my capacity to extend patience and compassion.

DESCRIBE YOUR VISION FOR AN IMPROVED WORLD.

One where we wake up and ask ourselves, "How am I going to engage with the world?"; whether reflecting and thinking about what's around us or igniting human connection and having conversations with the people

COLLAGE ART BY KELLETTE ELLIOTT

around us. In my vision for an improved world, I see people coming together, celebrating our differences while weaving connections through conversation and storytelling. Sharing our own stories is a big step, but equally important is the openness to listen and learn from the diverse experiences of others.

HOW HAS YOUR FAMILY SUPPORTED YOU?

My family has played a central role in my advocacy journey. Within a year of my coming out as transgender, we decided to open our home as a foster family for LGBTQ+ youth, a choice deeply influenced by our recognition of the need for loving and supportive environments. Witnessing my parents extend unconditional love to me and later to others illustrates the simplicity of acceptance and inclusivity, although it's far from easy or flawless. This experience has profoundly shaped my approach to advocacy, emphasizing the importance of valuing individuals for who they are and not solely making assumptions based on their labels or backgrounds.

WHAT ARE YOU CURRENTLY WORKING ON?

In addition to working on small projects and exploring new professional development opportunities, I'm also working on myself. This past year has been transformative for me as far as personal growth and exploration go. As a kid, I spent a lot of time asking questions and reflecting on my identity and who I was. When I finally found words corresponding with who I knew I was, I thought it was a done deal and that I finally "knew" myself. It took me a surprisingly long time to realize that my coming out as transgender at twelve was just the beginning of my journey of "self-discovery."

I've learned that "self-discovery" is not about reaching a destination or finding an answer but allowing yourself to embrace and enjoy the present freely. It is too easy to get caught up worrying about the future or finding a hobby, but what I know now is that self-discovery is an ongoing process! And that means trying new things! Whether diving into my studies, going to museums, enjoying nature walks, writing poetry, learning how to play the guitar, or meeting new people, I'm constantly learning and evolving. It's been a journey of reflection and understanding.

I'm learning to embrace my authentic self at a small and large scale while actively engaging with the world around me, breaking down barriers to build genuine connections. That said, lately, I've been experimenting with film as a powerful platform for storytelling and uplifting voices, eager to discover ways to ignite human connection and foster inclusivity. I've learned it's all about finding ways to motivate collaboration, ignite human connection, and dismantle the boundaries that hold us back from sharing our humanity.

interview:

OUR COVER ARTIST VALERIO VIDALI

VALERIO IS AN ITALIAN ILLUSTRATOR WHO CREATES ENCHANTING PICTURE BOOKS AND SPENDS HIS SPARE TIME BUILDING KITES THAT RARELY FLY.

Q: TELL US ABOUT A BOOK FROM CHILDHOOD THAT STILL INFLUENCES YOU TODAY.

A: In my childhood home, there were no picture books growing up, but I did have a 12-volume illustrated encyclopedia for young readers, which I loved and treasured (still do today!).

I adored the busy images and all the tiny details of the illustrations. I'm not sure if I can say that it has been an influence in my work, but it has certainly influenced the way I read and appreciate images.

The Shadow Elephant
Nadine Robert & Valerio Vidali

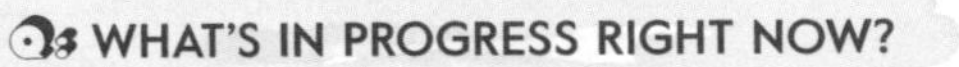

A: A small art book about tango. A big book about the history of people from generation to generation. And a couple of chairs I'm designing and building with a friend.

interview, continued

Q: TELL US ABOUT A DREAM PROJECT YOU'D LIKE TO LAND.

A: I would love to create the set design for a theater play or maybe a playground. I'm trying to find more three-dimensionality in my work.

Q: WHAT DO YOU DO WHEN THINGS GET DIFFICULT?

A: If I'm extremely frustrated with what I'm doing, then I'll stop working. In my experience, nothing is going to change if I keep working while feeling miserable. Usually, I go do something else—meet a friend, go for a walk, watch a movie, do some gardening, procrastinate—it doesn't really matter. I let time pass, recharge my batteries, and get back at it once I find a better outlook.

← scene from inside THE SHADOW ELEPHANT, written by Nadine Robert

Q: WHAT DID YOU IMAGINE YOU WOULD BE WHEN YOU GREW UP?

A: Early on, I remember wishing to be a dog, which unfortunately didn't happen. Then I thought I would become a veterinarian, fueled by my desire to be around dogs; but then I realized that veterinarians are doctors, and by then, I already knew that I didn't like school. Later, I thought I could be a comic book artist for Mickey Mouse.

Q ART SUPPLY YOU CAN'T LIVE WITHOUT?

A I'm terrible at taking care of my brushes, so I keep buying new ones.

Q FAVORITE SNACK WHILE WORKING?

A Parmesan, nuts, olives.

Q ALBUM LISTENED TO RECENTLY?

A *Miss America* by Mary Margaret O'Hara.

Q MORNING PERSON OR NIGHT OWL?

A Neither, early afternoon.

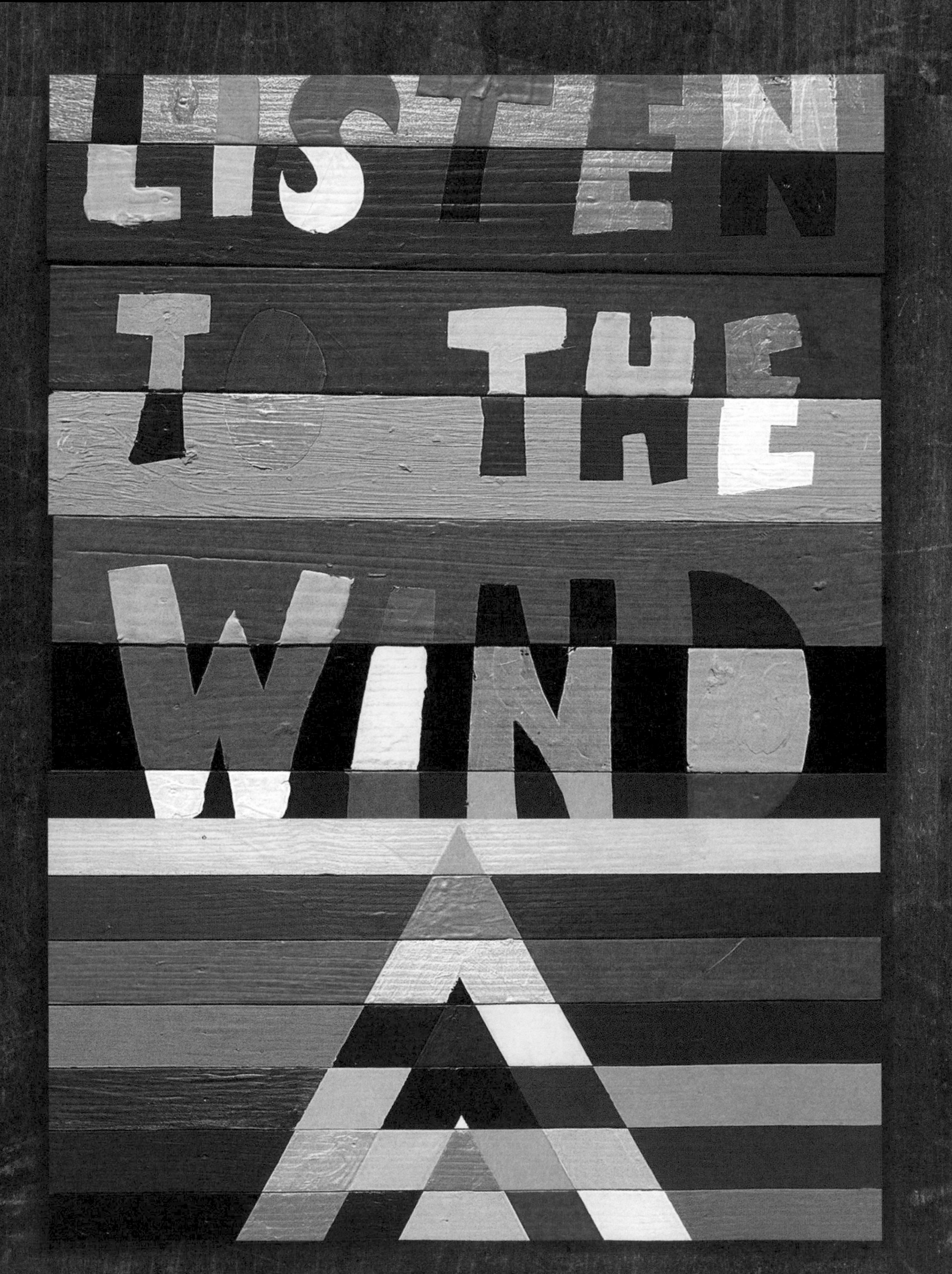
LISTEN
TO THE
WIND

OUR CHAPTER PAGES FEATURE ART BY LARRY YES (LEFT) AND ELEVATOR TEETH (RIGHT)

MAKE, DRAW, WRITE

Make this:
FAIRY BREAD
OFFICIAL Dog Chef RECIPE
By Tom Bingham
what you need:
3 SLICES OF BREAD
BUTTER
SPRINKLES!

BUTTER THE BREAD
CUT THE BREAD INTO HEART SHAPES
TIP!
USE A HEART SHAPED COOKIE CUTTER TO MAKE IT EASIER!
POUR THE SPRINKLES ONTO A PLATE
PRESS BREAD BUTTER SIDE DOWN INTO SPRINKLES
FLIP IT OVER AND ENJOY!
FRUITY OPTION:
TRY CUTTING HEARTS OF THIN SLICED APPLE AND USE CREAM CHEESE INSTEAD OF BUTTER

MAKE THIS WILD-FORAGED *paintbrushes*

with ELENIA BERETTA

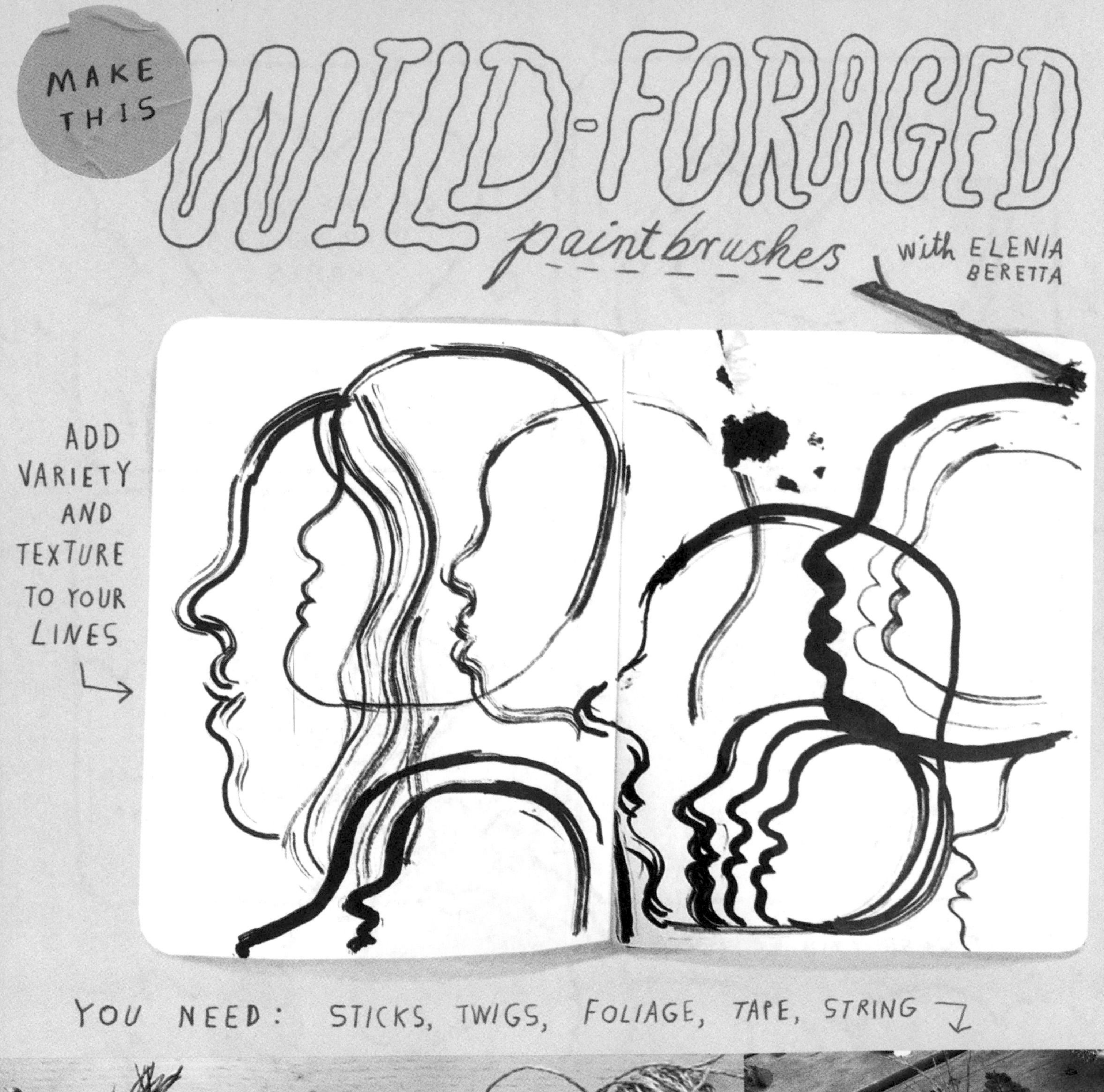
ADD VARIETY AND TEXTURE TO YOUR LINES

YOU NEED: STICKS, TWIGS, FOLIAGE, TAPE, STRING

PHOTOS FROM "DRAWING NIGHTS BERLIN" - WORKSHOP BY ELENIA BERETTA

1. TAKE A WALK IN A PARK OR YOUR YARD. GATHER BITS OF PLANTS FROM THE GROUND (OR ASK IF YOU CAN TRIM THE TIP OF A BRANCH.)
2. TAPE THE SMALLER PARTS TO THE END OF SOME TWIGS.
3. DIP INTO INK, AND DRAW.

WRITE THIS-
ANONYMOUS VALENTINE
MAKE SOMEONE'S DAY. MAYBE YOU DON'T KNOW THEM! MAYBE THEY DON'T KNOW YOU?
1. GRAB SOME PAPER SCRAPS, TRIM TO THE SIZE OF A CARD.
2. WRITE A LIST OF INTERESTING PHRASES (see below for ideas)
3. PICK ONE TO WRITE IN BOLD, COLORFUL LETTERING
4. LEAVE IT: FOR SOMEONE TO FIND
on a doorstep
on a car window
in a coffeeshop

WHERE TO GET IDEAS

FOR YOUR MYSTICAL POETIC ONE-SENTENCE MESSAGES?

What about song lyrics? → **YOU ARE MY SUNSHINE, MY ONLY SUNSHINE**

Or random lines from a poem → **WHAT ARE YOU GOING TO DO WITH YOUR ONE WILD AND BEAUTIFUL LIFE?** (by Mary Oliver)

Movie quote → **SOME PEOPLE ARE WORTH MELTING FOR** (guess which movie?)

DON'T YOU
LOVE PEOPLE
THAT ARE
LIKE A
WEIRD LITTLE
SECRET DOOR

↖ by artist KATIE BENN

DRAWN BY YOU
PROMPT: Draw your heart as a cartoon.
IAN, age 8, CALIFORNIA, USA
LOVE is the SECERT INGREDIENT
LUNA, age 7, BROOKLYN USA
FEDOR, age 11 LONDON, UK
When I am sad, I don't want to talk...
When I am happy, I want to sing!
CHIARA, age 8
PORTLAND, OR, USA
KAVYA, age 5
ATLANTA, GA, USA
LENA, age 7
VIRGINIA, USA

Ballet Heart
— Meredith, age 5
Mendon, Vermont
JUNIPER, age 7
HAWAII
FILIPPO, age 6, POLAND
?
GRR!!!
DUYAN, age 7
PHILIPPINES
by Zev
Age 9
PORTLAND
OREGON,
USA
LUCIE
age 5
SAN-
FRAN-
CISCO,
USA

WE ASKED STUDENTS TO DESCRIBE AN OBJECT THAT EVOKES AN EMOTIONAL MEMORY.

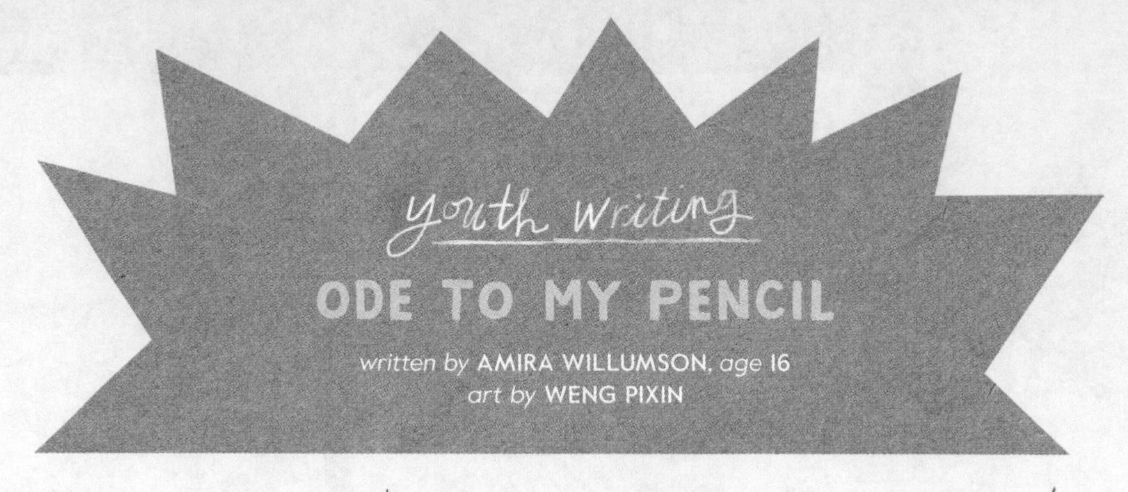

youth writing
ODE TO MY PENCIL
written by AMIRA WILLUMSON, age 16
art by WENG PIXIN

This is a writer's serenade to a pencil.

I am grateful that it has given me the power to cultivate my thinking and create something larger than myself. The simple pencil produces written life. It is the beholder of creation.

It gives voice to silence and
sheds light on darkness.

The pencil connects to my soul; dreaming.
It has given me the gift of expression.
Writing is the ritual we partake in, together.
The pencil graciously drafts my thoughts, dreams, and determinations.

Many notebooks and years have passed—
this pencil has kept me company
across many lifetimes.

This pencil has been like a lighthouse
in a weary storm, giving me hope.

from THE BUREAU OF FEARLESS IDEAS *in* SEATTLE, WASHINGTON
A MEMBER OF THE INTERNATIONAL ALLIANCE OF YOUTH WRITING CENTERS

PIXIN

WE ASKED STUDENTS TO DESCRIBE AN OBJECT THAT EVOKES AN EMOTIONAL MEMORY.

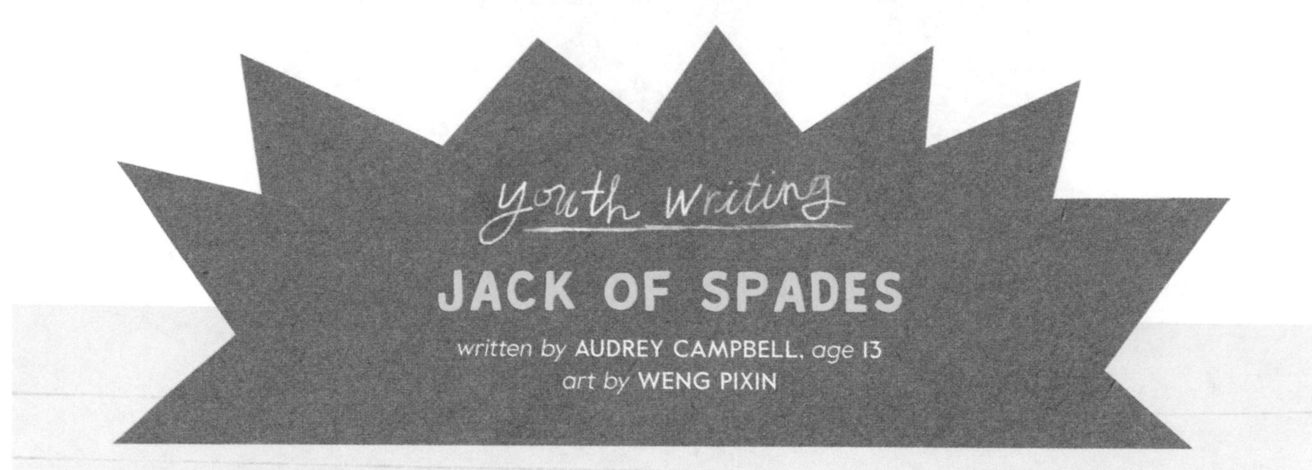

JACK OF SPADES

written by AUDREY CAMPBELL, *age* 13
art by WENG PIXIN

The world outside my window is painted gray. Tall evergreens shiver in the wind, sword-sharp pine needles falling to the ground, as dull light chokes on the waft of rain. I tug on the blinds and sink to the floor.

A drawer of memories. I sift through "First Day of School!" signs and old lanyards for events that no longer exist until I find what I am looking for.

A black leather pouch, hand-stitched and tattered from age. It's soft in my hands, like a feather. I open the flap and hear the jingle of metal on metal.

A folding cribbage board, with blue-backed cards and a creaking hinged compartment for six metallic pegs, three raven black, three silver as the moon. I trace my thumb over the hazelnut wood with a chocolate stripe down the middle. Dozens of tiny, drilled holes

in neat lines down each side. I twirl a silver peg and drift back in time. I am sitting at a wooden table, engulfed by the drip of rain on a peaceful lake and the soft clicking of solar-powered figurines, covering every square inch of the windowsill, waving to no one. The day's last breath of light lands on our faces in a beautiful ombre of pink, orange, and yellow. A ring of laughter floats through the air from the seat across from me. A flowered blouse, wired reading glasses, a buoyant smile. I am about to win for the fifth time, but my grandma isn't tired yet. Board games, card games, party games, it doesn't matter.

We play everything, after my dad gets bored and until we can't stay up any longer. Stories weave through every turn, a neighbor in the local paper years ago for getting a perfect hand in cribbage, a new book with a riveting plot, and the day's adventure in our little paradise. I sit smiling and hoping to never forget each second.

I lift my little silver peg and flash back to reality. I place it lightly and cut the deck. The best card, the jack of spades, stares back at me, but now, a year later and across the country, I am by myself in a hollow silence. I hear my exhale and the laundry machine's whir. I close the board and slide it back into its pouch and sit there holding it for a moment too long, taking in each red stitch, each imperfection, wishing the past to come back and grasping for a time just out of reach. With a sigh I place it back in its drawer, a moment frozen in time for another rainy day.

from THE BUREAU OF FEARLESS IDEAS *in* SEATTLE, WASHINGTON
A MEMBER OF THE INTERNATIONAL ALLIANCE OF YOUTH WRITING CENTERS

LOVE
YES
LOVE

LAUGH & PLAY

OUR CHAPTER PAGES FEATURE ART BY **LARRY YES** (LEFT) AND **ELEVATOR TEETH** (RIGHT).

REVIEW BY: IDA FROM HAWAI'I, AGE 9

BOOK BY BILL WATTERSON

"I recommend this book about a boy named Calvin and a tiger named Hobbes. Even though Hobbes is a stuffed tiger, that doesn't stop him from becoming a walking talking furry friend. They have a very strong relationship, Hobbes is always there for Calvin and Calvin is always there for Hobbes. This book makes me feel that even if I don't have anyone to talk to, I will always have Calvin and Hobbes."

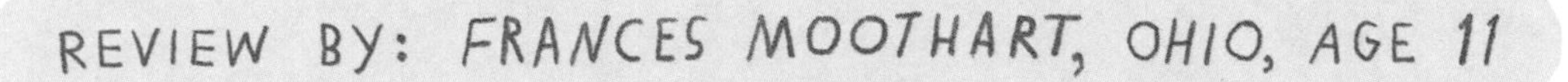

BOOK BY DEBORAH DIESEN

ON OUR PLAYLIST

Slow down and enjoy the soothing tunes of this folk album by Larry Yes (whose art graces our chapter pages in this issue!). We especially love the song ***NEW DAD RAG***, an ambient, peaceful welcoming of a child into the world.

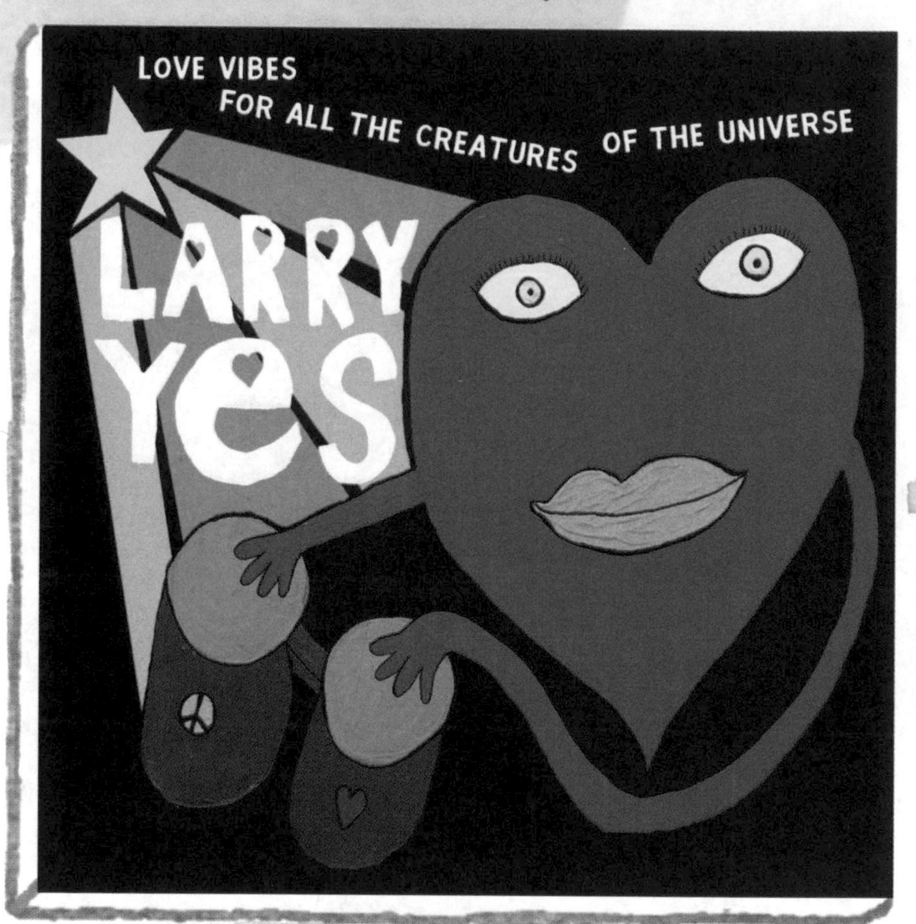

In the words of Lucky Brown, "Larry Yes is an artist who paints in broad strokes of bold, bright, vibrant, and pure colors. In the same way, his music is pure essences of messages of love for all the creatures of the universe… even the particles."

LISTEN TO OUR FULL PLAYLIST FOR THIS ISSUE ON SPOTIFY. USE THIS QR CODE TO DELVE INTO AN HOUR OF EAR-TINGLING TUNES… THE PERFECT BACKDROP TO JUMP INTO ONE OF THE DIY PROJECTS FROM CHAPTER 3.

ON OUR DESK:

recommended by our guest writers, Jessixa and Aaron Bagley.

Da Vinci Cosmotop Spin paintbrushes are my favorite because the handle has three sides-sides–like a triangle–so theyso they don't fall out of my fingers. And they are RED! ← from JESSIXA

From AARON:

I love this Charvin mini palette. It has all the colors I need and it is small so it doesn't clutter my table. I can throw it in my pocket and paint on the go!

I also love the Pentel brush pen filled with a thick purple ink so I can get a beautiful dry brush effect.

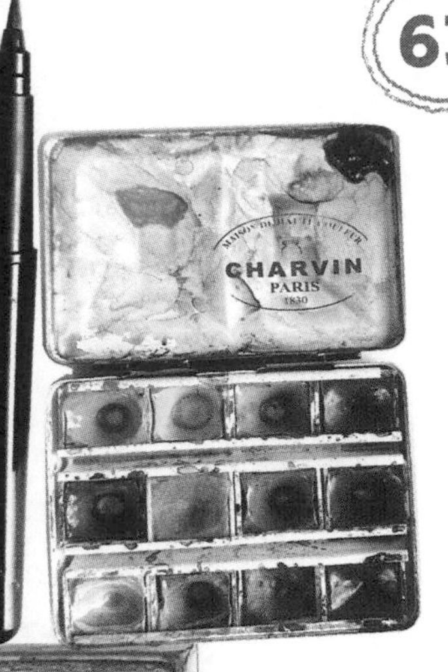

My palette has refillable paint pots and mixing surfaces! And I can just fold it up and take it on the go.

Eye droppers are fantastic for holding paint water to apply to the paper so you don't have to keep dipping your brush in the color.

FAV ✱ SNACKS!

TAPATIO DORITOS! They are SUPER hot and spicy and will turn my fingers red, so I can't eat them while working or else I'll get red all over my paper!

These lightly coated chocolate almonds are a great snack, though they do leave your fingers covered in powdery cocoa. Beware!

Like You, Like Me
From the award-winning creator of Same, Same but Different
Jenny Sue Kostecki-Shaw
Homemade LOVE
bell hooks
with pictures by Shane W. Evans

ON OUR BOOKSHELF

love of... all human beings

Portrait of a cross-cultural friendship, as told through exchanged letters.

-by JENNY SUE KOSTECKI-SHAW

Who better to explain the essence of love than bell hooks -- expert writer on matters of the heart? Here, she distills her wisdom for young readers.

-by BELL HOOKS

-art by SHANE W. EVANS

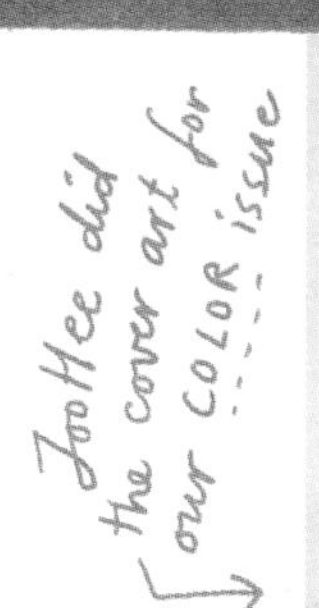

JooHee did the cover art for our COLOR issue

THE BOOK OF WHYS
GIANNI RODARI
Illustrated by JooHee Yoon
Translated from Italian by Antony Shugaar

If you know someone curious, this one is a must-read, or rather, a must-ponder!

love of... Questions

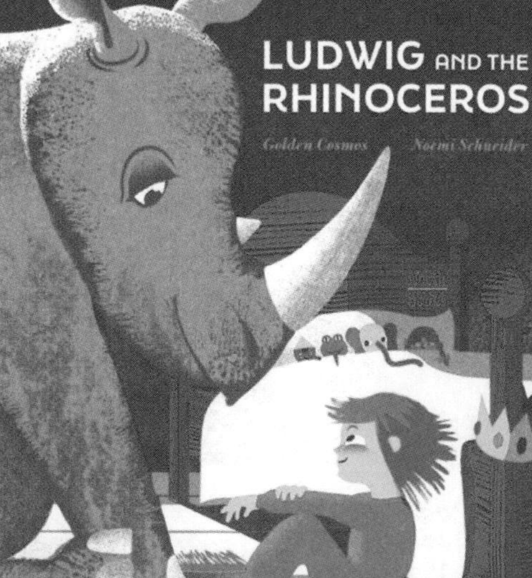

LUDWIG AND THE RHINOCEROS
Golden Cosmos
Noemi Schneider

This picture book explores a love of ... Philosophy!

If you've never understood this arena of inquiry before, an invisible blue rhino is waiting to explain it all.

-by GIANNI RODARI
-art by JOOHEE YOON

-by NOEMI SCHNEIDER
-art by GOLDEN COSMOS

really makes you think

TALES OF LOVE WE'VE BEEN READING!
Who doesn't love pizza? There are so many kinds! A tasty visual feast awaits all pizza fanatics, inside.
-by ELENIA BERETTA
WE LOVE PIZZA
Everything you want to know about your number one food
Elenia Beretta
LITTLE GESTALTEN
love of FOOD
NEW YORK TIMES bestseller
DRAGONS LOVE TACOS
by Adam Rubin
illustrated by Daniel Salmieri
How many tacos does it take to satisfy a dragon? Wait.... they eat tacos??????
-by ADAM RUBIN
-art by DANIEL SALMIERI
love and... creatures
-by MARIA POPOVA
-art by PING ZHU
Maria Popova
Ping Zhu
The Snail with the Right Heart
a true story
THE LION AND THE BIRD
MARIANNE DUBUC
-by INGRID CHABBERT
-art by GURIDI
THE DAY I BECAME A BIRD
INGRID CHABBERT
GURIDI
based on a true story
- by MARIANNE BUBUC
(this one is very funny)

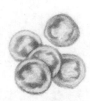

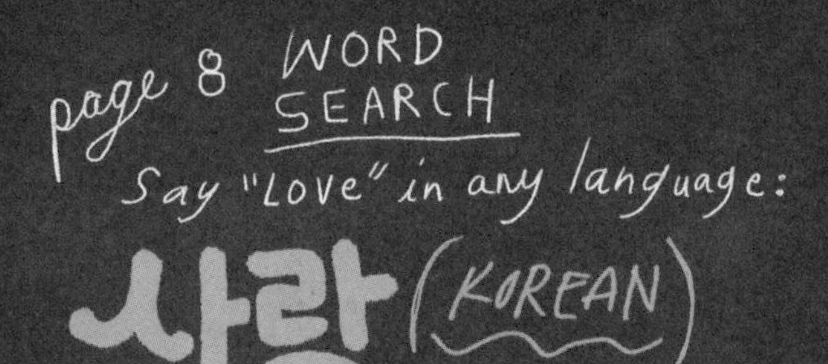

indifferentlanguages.com/words/love

CREATURE FEATURE

page 26 one-sided loves → Synanthropes

WHAT ARE THEY? MORE INFO

'Night of the Living Synanthropes'
by Allison Meier
Bloomberg CityLab, www.bloomberg.com

BLISTERING BARNACLES! HOW IS THAT LARGE RODENT RIDING AN ALLIGATOR?

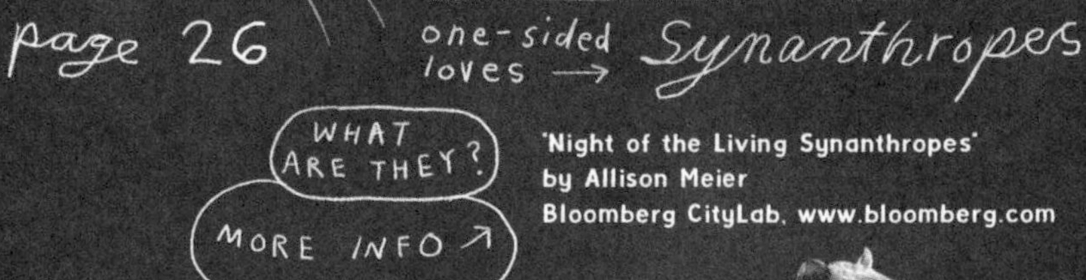

SMALL TALK: FACTOIDS, page 16

READ MORE STORIES IN THIS BOOK

Unlikely Loves: 43 Heartwarming True Stories from the Animal Kingdom
by Jennifer S. Holland

LOVE OF SWEET THINGS,

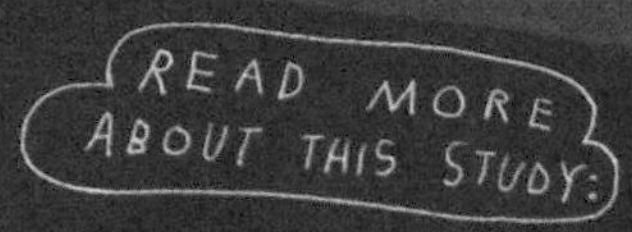
READ MORE
ABOUT THIS STUDY:

"Why Does Sugar Taste So Good?"
by Sabrina Stierwalt
scientificamerican.com

MAZE
page 13

page 24
WE ASKED A POET –
Where does
Love reside
in the Body?

MORE ABOUT HOW
THE HEART BECAME THE
SYMBOL FOR LOVE:

Listen to Marilyn Yalom's talk about the history of this: ideas.ted.com

page 8
WORD SLEUTH – answer key

SYNONYMS FOR LOVE

P G S E R
C X S D E M M Z U
B E S S H E Z V P Y Y
R U N C A R I N G T A T X
D K D U T Y F R L C S T I
F F E X T Z E X E M D V I H R
U R U G L D G Q S L Q I F Q Y
K S I A X W A E P O R B B V N
P P O E W V K V E V H E K F I
E Q W Y N H G F C E W S G Y T
M G U L D D X T X L R M W
X Y K T Q S B G W P Z Q F
K L O G P H H Z A J S
F I S O Y I T N J
C J J W P

THE YOUTH WRITING IN THIS ISSUE IS BY STUDENTS FROM:

The Bureau of Fearless Ideas
Seattle, Washington

TAKE A TRIP AND VISIT!

FIND A WRITING CENTER NEAR YOU: ➡ **YOUTHWRITING.ORG**

In every issue of Illustoria, students from the International Alliance of Youth Writing Centers contribute their own writing and art to add a range of voices to these pages. The International Alliance is joined in a common belief that young people need places where they can write and be heard, where they can have their voices polished, published, and amplified. There are nearly seventy centers worldwide. Learn more at www.youthwriting.org.